CATAPULTED

How Great Leaders
SUCCEED BEYOND
Their Experience

DAVE JENNINGS

MORGAN JAMES PUBLISHING • NEW YORK

CATAPULTED

ISBN: 978-1-60037-414-2 (Paperback)
ISBN: 978-1-60037-415-9 (Hardcover)

Library of Congress Control Number: 2008925061

Published by:

MORGAN · JAMES
THE ENTREPRENEURIAL PUBLISHER ™
www.morganjamespublishing.com

Morgan James Publishing, LLC
1225 Franklin Ave Ste 32
Garden City, NY 11530-1693
Toll Free 800-485-4943
www.MorganJamesPublishing.com

Cover/Interior Design by:
Rachel Lopez
rachel@r2cdesign.com

Habitat for Humanity®
Peninsula
Building Partner

LEADERS AT ALL LEVELS
EMBRACE *CATAPULTED*!

"Compelling ideas to help leaders rise to new levels of effectiveness."
VINCE MENDILLO, Director,
Microsoft

"Enjoyable to read and intimately applicable, *Catapulted* provided an opportune bridge from business school to corporate success by helping me find the key questions."
SAMUEL D. BERNARDS, Strategist,
WAL-MART

"Fantastic. Very clear and extremely applicable. Jennings really understands what leaders are going through. He makes the points quickly and concisely…His style allowed me to spend more time thinking about how to apply the principles…it's something that any manager or executive can read in a short amount of time. I loved Catapulted and will be buying copies and giving it to others… Every leader will find several gems in Catapulted."

JOHN MONTGOMERY, CFA, CPA , Investment Banking,

RBC Capital Markets, New York

"I love Catapulted. I found something meaningful and real on every page. It's unlike other leadership books in that it's so personal and accessible. It was refreshing to read through a leadership book that's truly honest, and that admits to some level of vulnerability! The story reminds leaders that it is all about problem-solving— intelligently winging it. Catapulted provides immediate insight for leaders at every level."

BROOKE MCILVAIN, HR Generalist,

Honeywell

"Catapulted moves leaders beyond the Peter Principle! Our managers, partners and entire firm will benefit from these insights on leadership. I recommend Catapulted for any manager looking to go to the next level."

ROBERT G. Moody, Jr., CPA

Talbot, Korvola & Warwick, LLP

"Wow does this story sound like my professional life. Catapulted captures the reality and challenges faced by managers on a daily basis. The lessons help leaders to look at their own assumptions and barriers in a new way. Excellent practical advice on how to grow and improve leadership capabilities. A great read."

CHUCK SIGMUND, Manager,
Organizational Development and Training
State Government

"Catapulted is engaging and aptly describes how managers can successfully navigate in today's highly turbulent and challenging global business world. It provides principles that serve as a roadmap for successfully managing career transitions that will to lead to business results! These principles resonated with me. I am absolutely sure they will resonate with any leader…at any level…in any business."

WINSOR JENKINS, Vice President, Human Resources,
Northwest Pipe Company
Author of "The Collaborator"

"You will want to pick up Catapulted many times for its wisdom and tools. Brings out the key questions leaders should be asking"

TENNESON WOOLF, Director,
William G. Dyer Institute for Leading Change

"All I can say is 'Wow!' A masterful leadership story that gets right to the heart and soul of the challenges that leaders at all levels experience every day. Dave provides a path to bring out our own unique expertise, perspective and sense of hope to answer the difficult questions of leadership. I can hardly wait to send copies to my colleagues."

KARL HUNRICK, President,

ThinkTank

I absolutely love it!! The story is readable and interesting while the concepts are approachable and actionable. Dave's many years of experience working with leaders shows throughout Catapulted. I already have many clients I'm dying to give books to!!

MARIO RAIA, President,

Combined IQ

"Very Engaging! Catapulted weaves a story that will change the way you look at and approach business critical situations. Practical tools every leader must understand to be successful. Catapulted will cause you to ask critical questions that will bring your leadership to a higher level. I recommend this book to anyone looking to succeed as a leader."

TABER RIGG, Assistant Manager,

General Mills

"Catapulted provides great insights for leaders at all levels of an organization. Catapulted gives leaders an ongoing renewal process—helping them remain resilient and adaptable through more and more complex demands."

JOHN COCHRAN, President,

Executive Forum

TABLE OF CONTENTS

PREFACE

As a leader, you are constantly thrown beyond your experience. It doesn't matter if you are a Fortune 500 CEO, a department manager, or the PTA president. The situation is the same. When you accept the responsibility to lead, you discover the job is bigger than your experience. This has always been true.

However, what's different in today's economy is the expectation for you to perform at higher levels sooner—much sooner.

This demand is caused by several factors. First, the complexity of today's organizations has created a steeper learning curve. So, you not only have to think about budgeting, scheduling, and planning, you also have to think politically, environmentally, and globally. And, even if your company isn't global, your customer's company probably is.

Second, thirty-five percent of the workforce is expected to retire during the next ten years. This exodus has already created holes in leadership. The sheer number of leadership opportunities is greater than the supply of leaders.

Third, organizational tenure is shorter. Switching companies is more common for you, your boss, and your employees. Thus, company knowledge is no longer maintained. You must spend more time learning, aligning, and influencing to get the same things done.

These and other trends are contributing to the fact that over 40 percent of companies worldwide are unable to find qualified leaders. Additionally, the shortage of prepared leaders has made managerial and executive jobs ranked as one of the top ten jobs needing more people.

So, what can you do in this new world? How can you more quickly fill the widening gap between demands and experience? How can you step up and lead at the next level? The answer is found within *Catapulted: How great leaders succeed beyond their experience.*

Catapulted provides you a path to enhance your mindset and your skill set. You gain a new perspective on how to approach your job and proven tools to do your job.

To embrace the spirit of leaving your comfort zone, *Catapulted* is told as a leadership parable. The main character is a manufacturing manager named Stan. He is promoted into a crisis and is wondering why he ever took the job. He is expected to make critical decisions without complete information. And, in the midst of all his challenges, he can't get over the feeling that he is just faking his way through management. Stan must discover where to focus his energy before time runs out.

Stan's story is based on the experience of thousands of leaders who stepped up to embrace the real job of leadership. Stan is waiting to tell you his story—the story you share with every leader.

CHAPTER 1 ······················▶

Meet Stan

Because I'm the manager, people think I know about a lot of things. So, I make things up as I go: answers in staff meetings, predictions about the next year, and estimates on budget.

It's not exactly *lying*. It's closer to making an educated guess—on something I'm not educated about. I'm supposed to know, so I act like I do. It takes a lot of energy.

It isn't just work that people expect me to know about. I've got employees who ask me how to raise kids, buy a car, select a major, choose a house, and know if they are in love.

They seem to think I have a corner on the future. What a funny position to be in. I haven't figured out for myself half the things they want me to solve for them. Sometimes it is an ego boost. Sometimes it is a drain.

If I were really honest with myself, I would have to say that sometimes—even a lot of times—I don't really know what in the world I am doing. I keep wondering when my boss will realize I am just faking it.

For me, being a manager is like taking someone else's identity and seeing how long I can maintain the charade. I often question how long it will be before someone figures out that I don't really know what I am doing.

I sometimes wonder when the leadership police will surround my office and tell me to come out with my hands up so that no one will get hurt. I then come out peacefully, and they parade me in handcuffs through my colleagues. The police charge me with impersonating a leader and put me in jail, so I can't hurt anybody.

I used to think leaders were these people who were confident, inspiring, and knowledgeable. Nowadays, I look in the mirror, and I see me—just me. I have weeds in my lawn, kids who talk back, and credit card challenges. And, I don't own a crystal ball that tells me what we should do next at work.

I didn't start off expecting to be in this exact position. In fact, I really enjoyed most of the things I was doing in my old job—

solving problems, figuring out the details, and seeing things get finished! I enjoyed the expertise and respect I had gained in my last job. I felt like I knew what I was doing.

Nowadays, there are so many more people to stay connected with and so many more changes and ambiguities. There is less control of more things.

In this job, I don't have time to do any of the good stuff I'm supposed to do as a manager. You know—be strategic, coach, listen, develop, inspire, etc. Hah! I've got so many fires to put out that I hardly have time for any of that stuff. I think survival is really underrated.

Sometimes, I think I spend so much time on the details that I don't have time for the decision making. I am supposed to make great decisions. But, I rarely have even 20 percent of the information I wish I had to make a good decision. If I take the time to get good information, the opportune moment has passed.

I also have the challenge, or should I say trauma, of proposing new ideas to management. I am not sure if it is more frightening to have my proposals accepted or turned down.

On the one hand, I have to deliver on tremendous claims that I made—claims that even I question we can handle. There is always that question inside me, "What if I convince them to invest big dollars, and then I am wrong?"

On the other hand, I question if I am adding any value when no one is willing to listen to my ideas. Maybe they really don't need me here.

I once told my boss that I really wonder if I made the right decision to take this job. She told me that it is common to feel that way, and I'd figure it out. She said she hired me not because I know everything but because she believed I could learn what to do. I just hope my learning curve catches up with the demands of work.

CHAPTER 2

The Bad News

"Hello, Stan. This is Blanche. I need you to come up to Bob's office for a few minutes," the president's secretary casually states over the phone. "Oh, and by the way, your boss is in the meeting, too."

"I will be right up."

Oh, great! I'm here for fifteen minutes this morning, and the president of the company wants to see me. What in the world can he want? The only time he calls me is when something is really wrong. Why doesn't my boss let me know what is going on? Why is my boss in his office?

"Hi, Bob. Hi, Heather," I voice as I walk into Bob's office.

"Hi, Stan. Come on in," Bob shakes my hand as we both sit at the table. "Thanks for coming up so quickly."

"Hello, Stan," Heather, my boss, nods and smiles at me as if she definitely knows something that I don't.

"If HR were here I would assume this was a termination meeting," I say half jokingly and half wondering if it were true.

"Well, I won't beat around the bush." Bob smiles at my comment but gets right to his point. "Sanlar Technologies is threatening to pull their business. They want us to lower our price."

"What do you mean? They have been a loyal customer for the last four years. They love what we do for them. They have been one of our references for potential clients," I speak with shock.

"I know. But, they have a new VP of Operations over there, and he insists that they put all of the major contracts out to bid," Bob responds. "They have three bids lower than ours, and they are asking us to match the medium bid."

"But lowering up-front costs isn't going to save them any money in the long run. It's not just the upfront costs. It's the quality and service we provide throughout the year," I add.

"I know that, you're preaching to the choir," Bob acknowledges. "But, here's the deal. If we don't get this contract, a lot of things will change. First, we will completely miss this quarter's earnings. Second, our expansion will have to be stopped. And third, we will probably have to lay some people off."

"And, just as bad, if we do get the contract, we could be in a lot of trouble servicing it," Heather adds. "We could lose on the front end and the back end. Additionally, our quality of service and our contracts with other companies would be threatened by requests for cuts. You know that information would get out quickly. And besides, we can't service the account without the current margin levels. It isn't like we have been getting rich on his account."

"Yes, Heather. You are quite right," Bob confirms and turns back to me.

"Stan, I called you in because Heather says you have the best relationship with Blake, Sanlar's operation's manager," Bob continues. "I met with their VP yesterday, and he doesn't seem to be budging on anything. I am hoping you can make some headway and get at the bottom of what they need, so we can make a realistic deal. Also, I want you and Heather to do an estimate from an operations point of view about what it would cost us to accept Sanlar's offer. Our final meeting with Sanlar Technologies is in three weeks. Our executive team will meet in two weeks to decide if we can afford to turn them down. I know you and Heather will have lots of work to pull together by then. Your input will have a major impact on the direction we take. If you need anything, or anyone, just let me know."

"Well, how far can we go on this? We have a lot to lose. Can we really say no?" I ask, trying to figure out if I have any real power to decide.

"That is the question I need the team to answer. I expect that we will be looking at layoffs if we turn down the contract. However, I really don't know what the answer should be until we get all the numbers from all of the departments," Bob resolutely responds.

I don't know whether to fake confidence, run away from home, or roll up in the fetal position and die. Bob thinks I have some special connection that is going to open the door to this whole thing. Sure, I've done work over there with Blake, but I don't think I have the depth of connection that he thinks I have.

I feel as if the company's viability is in my hands, and I have only been in this job for six months. I only have a few days to meet with Blake and get all the data together.

CHAPTER 3 .... *A Telegram*

The last couple of days have been nonstop adrenaline. Pulling together all the data for this Sanlar crisis is all-consuming. I'm glad to get out of the office and have time to slow down over the weekend.

My favorite way to put on the brakes is to check out antique shops. I always hope I will find something of unique value. It all seems so intriguing and different from my fast-paced world of management.

I shuffle through the aisles and find an interesting chest. The antiquity of the chest has its own appeal—worn leather straps, faded paint, rusty hinges, and the smell of attics, cellars, and dust.

I pull the lid back and begin to filter through the leather-bound books, pottery, and metal objects. I don't even know what some of this stuff is. Still, I like it.

I pick up the items and wonder where they all came from. How many people across the centuries have touched them?

I continue to survey this wooden time capsule, and one of the books catches my attention. It seems not just old but well used. As I carefully examine its worn pages, a paper falls to the floor, landing upside down. I guess it must be a bookmark. It isn't. Or, at least, it wasn't initially.

It is an old telegram. Discolored from years of aging, the note looks about fifty years old. The faded typed words simply read:

```
Alfred. Your presence requested. No. 16
Fleet Street. London. By April 30. History
affected by your decision. Bring the book.
Sanjay
```

What a note! I wonder who Alfred was. I bet he was in shock. Well, I guess he saved the world—we are still here. I wonder what happened to this Alfred guy.

Looking closer at the telegram, I notice a hand written note in faded black ink: "Why me?"

The meaning of the telegram consumes me so much that I lose

interest in the rest of the contents of the chest. After thinking a few minutes about the note, my thoughts return to the book. I wonder if this was the book he was supposed to bring.

I look at where the paper had been. The imprint of the telegram created a dent in the pages that surrounded it. It created a safe place to protect the note and keep it hidden from the world for many years. Maybe there was something important about where the note was in the book. I wish I could read the book, but it is in Latin or Greek or something.

My cell phone rings before I can look further at the book. The ring jolts me out of the possibilities and mystery of the telegram. I have been so consumed with the past that I had forgotten for a moment all the things I have to do.

"Hello, this is Stan... What do you mean the factory line is down? Okay, I'll be down there in about forty-five minutes. Go ahead and call the vendor, and get a service guy sent out."

At times like this, I sometimes wonder "why me?" I purchase the book and head to the factory.

CHAPTER 4

The Invitation

The last week has passed by like a dream. More fires to put out, more meetings, more conflicts, and, of course, more deadlines. Making estimates for the Sanlar bid is overwhelming.

Yet, that crazy old telegram has been consuming my thoughts more than the demands. When I sit at my desk, when I participate in a meeting, or even when I'm talking to someone, my mind drifts to that telegram. I can't get it off my mind. Was that invitation a hoax or did something really happen?

"Hi, Stan."

"Hi, Mark."

"This envelope was left for you at the reception desk. It looks like a telegram. What happened? Did you run out of money and call your mommy for a loan?" Mark teases.

"Oh, you are very funny, aren't you? Nobody is sending me any money. Give me the stupid letter and get out of here," I reply with a smile.

Mark is right. It is a telegram addressed to me. Who in the world sends a telegram these days? They quit sending telegrams several years ago. However, before I can come to a conclusion, I open it and start to read.

```
Stan. Your presence requested. No. 16
Fleet Street. London. By April 30. History
affected by your decision. Bring the book.
Alfred
```

The message makes my jaw drop. This is really strange. This is the same telegram.

Oh, I get it. Somebody has got to be playing a trick on me. Maybe it is one of my employees. Maybe it is one of the other managers. Maybe it is my wife.

But maybe, just maybe, this could be for real. But, it doesn't make any sense. Why in the world would any one want *me* to go do anything that would change history? I'm happy right here just doing my thing.

I pull out the original telegram and lay it next to the new telegram for confirmation. Everything on the new telegram is the same except for names and the handwritten note.

The telegram in the book is definitely old. It can't be a fake. Whoever received the old one was now sending it to me.

Maybe I should go to London. But to go over there I would have to take time off work and buy an expensive plane ticket. Then again, maybe I could take a few days off work. I'm sure I haven't used up much vacation time since becoming a manager.

Hold on! How can I even think of doing this in the middle of this Sanlar crisis? Even if the Sanlar crisis wasn't going on, who has time to take a break when you're a manager?

What am I thinking? I get an invitation in a telegram from somebody I don't know to go to some unknown place, and I am considering doing this? I have lost more marbles than I thought.

Yet, there is no way someone could have faked this note. I didn't tell anyone about the note except my wife, and I really don't think she would do this. But then who could have sent it?

CHAPTER 5 ..... *The Decision*

I can't believe this. I'm in the middle of London trying to find an address I received in a telegram from someone I don't even know. I really must be crazy.

The smells of a recent rain and food shops permeate the air. The people are supposedly speaking English, but I can hardly understand them. Everybody is driving on the wrong side of the road.

After fourteen hours of taxis, planes, and layovers, my head is foggy from jetlag, and I have no clue where I'm really going. The only thing I do have is a hope—a deep hope inside me that this may matter.

The last week of work is a blur. I met with Blake but made no progress. Heather and I pulled together the numbers before I left.

I told Heather that I needed to use some vacation for an extended weekend. Because we got our numbers in and the decision meeting isn't until next Thursday, she didn't seem to think much of me taking time off. Anyway, she has my cell phone if she needs anything.

I didn't dare tell her or anyone else what I was doing. Even now I stand the chance of being the laughing stock of the whole company. They are probably sitting back there laughing at my naivety to think I was selected to make a difference.

I am investing my money, my time, my ego, and my sanity in this. My wife supports me and feels the intrigue of the invitation. As we both tried to come up with all the reasons this was a hoax, we both came back to "what if it is for real?" We considered degrees of worst case and best case.

Worst case: I never go, and I always wonder if I should have. I second guess myself on everything I do for the rest of my life. I spend every empty moment staring into space wondering what would have happened if I would have tried. Not a good choice.

Next worst case: I go, and it is a setup. I make a fool of myself. Everyone is in on the joke, and I can't show my face at work ever again. I'm so embarrassed that I get a new job somewhere else (in another state and in a different industry). I spend my life worrying that someone will come up out of the crowd and say "Hey, are you the fool who thought he could make a difference?" Costly and emotionally painful, but survivable.

Next-next worst case: I get there, and it is some kind of trap. They take me hostage, and no one can afford to pay the ransom. So, they torture me. I die a slow, ignoble death. My wife misses me but is able to live happily on my life insurance policy. Strangely, I think I like this scenario better than being a fool.

Next-next-next worst case: I get there and nothing and no one is there. I waste my time and money. I think I'm a bit of a fool, but at least I know that I was willing to take a risk.

Better case: I get there. Nothing is like I imagine, but it is something interesting. I learn about another part of the world. I have an interesting adventure. I see some new things, try some interesting food, check out some antique shops... on second thought, if this doesn't turn out to be something, I'm not sure that I'll ever look at anything old again. But I feel good about taking a risk even though I am disappointed that I don't really have much to do with making things better in the world.

Best case: I get there, and it is something that really matters. I influence something of importance to some group of people—or maybe even the world. I gain confidence in trusting myself and taking risks. The future and history are changed. Everyone sees me as some superstar for taking the risk, I am on the cover of every major magazine, I get rich and... okay, maybe I'm getting carried away. But, hey, what if it matters?

The possibility of the best case, despite the dread of the worst case, somehow makes this worth trying. Deciding to come here wasn't very different from deciding to be a manager. I didn't really know what would happen then either.

So, here I am—a few blocks from the truth about my decision. In spite of all the doubts and not knowing exactly what will happen next, I feel confident—well, at least hopeful. My heart races as I turn the corner. I am anxious to discover my destiny at No. 16 Fleet Street.

CHAPTER 6
The Mentor

The large cloudy windows rising before me reveal the treasures of days gone by. This is an old book shop: Wildly & Co. Books and Collectibles, Established 1830.

I traveled five thousand miles to go to a book shop? Here I thought I had arrived at a crossroads, and it is just... just another store.

As I scan the contents of the shop through the window, I see nothing inside that makes me want to take the next step towards the door. Once I cross that threshold, my doubts about my judgment and my abilities might be confirmed.

A large part of me just wants to go back—back to my familiar world. If I just leave now, maybe I could forget I ever took such a quixotic adventure. If I stop now, I don't have to know the magnitude of my mistake.

But what did I expect? A brass band announcing my arrival... a welcoming committee... the trump of angels?

I guess I *was* expecting something. I just don't know what it was. But, I know I expected something more for my decision than a bunch of old books.

I guess if I were really honest with myself, I really hoped I was going to make a difference. I imagined that I had come to a point that I could really influence the future. I imagined someone had seen my full potential and was giving me a chance to use it. I imagined I would be doing something of value—something bigger than myself.

With a deep breath and while biting my lower lip, I pull on the doorknob and enter the store. The smell of old permeates the air. The wooden shelves tower up to the ceiling. A rolling ladder hangs down, waiting to be used.

The room is filled with hundreds, maybe thousands, of books, relics, and paintings. Dusty leather-bound books cover the shelves, the floor, the counter, and the windowsill. The overstuffed room holds more books than the shop was ever intended to hold. There is also a chest on the floor—similar to the chest I discovered back home.

Even without the band, welcoming committee, or the angels, I have to say that this is one interesting place. This collection of thoughts and history is inspiring, without even looking inside the covers. The quiet in the room is such a contrast to the busy pace of Fleet Street.

Yet, my temporary feeling of awe is relinquished to the reality that there isn't something more to the place. After gaining a moment of reluctant confidence, I call out, "Anyone here?"

Momentarily, a composed elderly man comes out through a squeaky door. I wonder if he has been around as long as some of the books. He warmly greets me and asks if I had any trouble finding the place. I wonder for a second if he knows who I am. I surrender the thought and answer his question with a generic, "No."

He asks how he can help me. I ponder if I should show him the telegram. Fearing the embarrassment of a lifetime, I consider keeping a low profile by casually responding that "I am just looking." However, reason leaves me, and I go ahead and place the telegram on the table in as nonexpectant a manner as I can muster.

He looks down and pauses. I watch him closely—looking for a ray of purpose in his eyes or posture.

He looks up slowly—way too slowly—and his calm, aged eyes provide me with the first moment of real hope I have had in the last week.

"I'm delighted you made the decision," he warmly shares. "You have just made one of the most important decisions of your life. I'm Alfred. Please, follow me back into the vault."

Though we have just met, I follow him like a trusted friend. We pass through the squeaky door and move decidedly beyond stacks of more books. His purposefulness and acceptance make me want to follow him anywhere. For a few moments, fear and doubt leave me completely. It is as if I have come home.

The private hallway is filled with more history—relics, paintings, and more books. We turn right and proceed down a set of solid stone stairs that are heavily worn. I can't image how many years the stairs have been here or how many feet have passed this way to wear the stones steps so smooth.

A door across from the last step is framed by more books and relics. He pulls out a key and opens the door. As we cross the threshold, we leave behind the haphazard placement of books and enter a room of order and brightness.

I feel like I am in a museum—books neatly resting on shelves, papyri in glass cases, and engraved metal plates on the wall. In one corner of the room are some carved stones. Alfred closes the door behind us and smiles.

"Marvelous, isn't it? It is the most magnificent collection of its kind in the world," the confident old Englishman beams without any arrogance.

"It's beautiful!"

"These papyri over here date back to 3300 BC. These brass plates are older than those belonging to King Darius. Some researchers say these scrolls over here were pulled from the Alexandria library before it was destroyed.

"This library is focused on one thing—leadership. Among these many majestic pieces of history are simple diaries and stories of leaders—good and bad, known and unknown. We have been collecting their successes and failures for centuries.

"I'm sure you wonder how it all began."

CHAPTER 7
The History

"About three thousand years ago, Tyre was the crossroads of the world. It was a Phoenician port city just south of Sidon—a place where desert and sea met. In its heyday, it was the New York City of its time—a busy port that was the center of industry and trade.

"Tyre was most famous for producing dye for the color purple. Tyrean purple was costly and worn as the mark of royalty. Thus, its reputation was known around the world.

"In this city, there was a young man named Tallis. He was a dutiful worker who became quite expert at his trade through much persistence.

"His faithful stewardship to oversee the storehouse was noticed by those above him and by leaders of the many caravans and ships that arrived in Tyre. Through the years, various leaders beckoned him to come and work for them, but he had become quite adept in his familiar world and refused their invitations.

"One day, the great merchant Aziz urged Tallis to come work for him as his assistant in overseeing an entire caravan. Aziz was known throughout the land as the common man who had achieved greatness without family ties or riches. To receive this invitation from him was an exceedingly great honor and opportunity.

"However, for Tallis, the opportunity was quite a leap, and caused him to question his ability. That night, after much discussion, Tallis convinced his wife *and* himself that he should take the risk.

"Tallis took the job but soon found that this challenge was not what he expected. The skillfulness by which he executed his old job as overseer did not transfer to the demands of his new responsibilities.

"He soon began to flounder—doubting himself and cursing his circumstances. He feared telling anyone of his needs because he did not want others to think him weak or incapable. After all, they had asked him to do this because of his great abilities.

"Convinced that his work could be accomplished if he just put in a little more time, he began to work a little more and more each night until he was spending all his time on his tasks.

"He was afraid to let anyone else do anything because, in his mind, they were all either too slow or too busy. But, his fears were costly. Some of his apprentices left for the caravans of the competitors. Others enjoyed the leisure they were offered by a leader who was willing to do so many tasks.

"Tallis had become like an ox that continued to carry its yoke even though the journey was over. He had become so comfortable with his previous expertise that he had forgotten the path he had walked to achieve mastery.

"He began to steal more and more time from his family to fulfill what he thought was his job. However, his philanthropy at work created emotional poverty in his home.

"His frustrations grew, and he began to wonder if he was indeed a failure. He often dreamed of being back in his old job where he felt valued and knew the rewards of his labors.

"One evening, as he left his work, he felt overwhelmingly condemned by the very job he thought would bring him opportunity and prosperity. He walked slowly through the streets, noticing the expertise of others and seeing only the failures and shortcomings within himself.

"The burdens of his work troubled him so much that he crumbled onto the stairs of one of the great halls of the city. Although he didn't know it, this was one of the most important falls of his life.

"He buried his head in his hands. He cursed himself as every doubt filled his mind. Why did he ever think he could do this? How could he continue to do his work so poorly?

"As he rubbed his tear-filled eyes, he looked upward at the entry of the great hall, and there etched in the marble walls and illuminated by the setting sun were these words:

ANSWER THE QUESTION OF YOUR TIME.

"He repeated the words to himself, but they meant nothing to him. However, as he continued to bemoan his circumstances the words returned: 'Answer the question of your time.'

"He thought whimsically, 'the only question I need answered is how do I get myself out of this quandary?'

"Fortunately, the thought interrupted his self pity to the point that he asked, 'What question do I need to answer during my time as a leader?' He paused and began to entertain this new question. As he considered the possibilities, he gained a moment of energy and continued his journey home.

"That evening he kept asking himself, 'What is the question I must answer during my time as a leader?'

"When he returned to work the next day, he continued to ask himself questions as he did his work. Each interaction of his day prompted a different question. 'How is it that Aziz has entrusted me with such responsibility while I cannot trust others? Why do the caravan workers spend so much time on the wrong things? Why are some merchants and customers willing to give me their time freely while others never have time for me? What is it that Aziz really rewards? What will make our caravan the most profitable? Why am I here long after the workers have returned to their families?'

"With each question, he asked himself if this was the question he must answer. But, not one of the questions seemed to ring true," Alfred pauses.

"So, how in the world did he figure out what he was supposed to focus on," I interrupt.

"That is an important question," Alfred responds and quickly continues. "Tallis extended his search beyond himself. He asked caravan masters, workers, customers, and Aziz what were the most important problems that had to be solved. As he listened to their concerns, he found they shared many common concerns but no consensus. He wrestled with all their comments and searched inside himself for the greater question. He soon realized that the biggest question facing *him* was how to reduce the loss of caravans due to bandits and inclement weather.

"He dedicated himself to finding an answer to this question. After much work, he greatly reduced the loss of the caravans on the road and then he moved on to finding a new question.

"His diligence in seeking and answering questions led him to success for himself and others; so, he strived to share his insights with anyone who was willing to learn. He wrote many of his thoughts, and he started collecting the writings of leaders from around the world. The collection you see here today started with just a few letters. Before he died, he left a charge to maintain, collect, and share the experiences of leaders with all leaders who are willing to learn.

"The location of this library has moved many times over the centuries, but it has been here in England for over five hundred years. The library was moved to this building about one hundred and fifty years ago. I received the charge to oversee these records some forty-five years ago.

"Like those before me, I constantly search out new archeological finds and even the current best sellers to see what should be added to the archive.

"However, in spite of all the new writings and the archeological discoveries, some of the most prized documents are the actual letters written by Tallis.

"Come, let me show you his letters." Alfred finishes and leads me across the room.

CHAPTER 8

The Challenge

"This glass case here contains the original letters written by Tallis on papyrus," Alfred comments with his English accent putting emphasis on papyrus. "They were written in response to the concerns of one of his leaders. We do not know the exact questions the leader asked Tallis. But, we do know that Tallis provided guidance on choosing a destination, clarifying values, cultivating relationships, and creating accountability."

"They look impressive. They must be worth a fortune," I voice.

"The antiquity of the letters alone places a high monetary value on these documents," Alfred speaks purposefully. "However, learning and applying the teachings is where the real, and indeed exponential, value is created. These letters have changed lives and organizations. And yes, even changed history."

"How many are there?" I question.

"We have four complete letters and fragments of a few others. However, the important question is not how many there are but how many apply to your current situation," Alfred speaks as he looks me in the eye. "Leadership is not about answering all questions. It is about answering the questions for your situation. These letters can help, but they never replace the need for you to identify the most critical questions of your time."

"So, how do I fit into all of this? Am I supposed to take your place here and keep this going?"

"Oh, no... no, my good man. On the contrary, it's time to look forward and move to the next level," he responds adamantly. "You see, too many leaders accept a new title, but very few accept the terms of the offer. They fail to discover what question they are really trying to answer and spend their time being busy but not truly productive."

"Well, I have sure seen a few leaders do that. They run from meeting to meeting waving their hands a lot and pounding their fist, but in the end nothing changes," I agree.

"Precisely! It takes great effort to focus on the right things."

"So, what *are* you asking me to do?" I ask.

"You need to determine the key question of your time as a leader and find your answer. These letters from Tallis can help you on your search."

"Well, can I read them and give you my answers now?" I request.

"You underestimate your challenge. Reading the letters provides insights on questions that need to be answered—no matter the situation. In fact, sometimes the letters may actually provide you the question of your time. However, you cannot fully answer the questions without input from your business partners.

"So, although you will begin your answers today, you must return to work to complete them. And remember, answering is not a single effort. As circumstances change, you will need to rediscover the question of your time.

"I have here an English translation of the letters that was written on parchment a few hundred years ago. This first letter will help you choose a destination. Take your time to read it. If you hastily read through the letter, you may miss out on the subtle ways the words apply to you. Please sit down over here. I will return in a few minutes to answer any questions."

CHAPTER 9
The First Letter

I get comfortable in a worn leather chair in the corner of the vault. Alfred leaves the room and the subdued light inside the display cases creates a gold hue across the room. The room feels very still at this moment.

I am rather surprised Alfred entrusts me with something of such antiquity. Just touching it feels extraordinary. I begin to read and the artifacts around me vanish from my consciousness.

My colleague and friend,

Your concerns about choosing a destination cause me to reminisce on my own journey. I can do no more than offer you my experience.

I started out as a common worker and arrived here after much hard work and many mistakes. I had no special gift. I could not predict the future. I was not smarter because of my new position.

I frequently questioned if I was choosing the right path. It seemed that each decision carried the weight of many oxen. Fortunately, I soon discovered that I did not have to carry such a heavy load. Leaders far wiser than I have struggled to know the right direction and encountered both successes and failures. If none of them had mastered tomorrow, why must I carry this burden of making a perfect choice? If I could predict the future, I would not need this job.

I found that to create the future, I had to make more time for it. I had to stop reacting to the everyday tasks that kept me busy and begin initiating conversations that gave me insight. I began talking with those who did the work. I began talking with those who supported the work. I began talking with those who demanded the work. And I began talking with those who bought the work. Then, I began making time for myself to make decisions.

Yet, in spite of my newfound knowledge, deciding was always difficult. My excuses to avoid decisions flowed more freely than the spring floods. I avoided deciding because I was too busy with the burdens of the moment. I avoided deciding because I was waiting for another's decision. But above all, I avoided deciding because I was afraid—afraid I could not live with my mistakes. Once I learned that I could survive the consequences of my choices, I became free to learn the lessons—both good and bad—of my experiences.

Now my friend, consider yourself as if you stood at the head of a delta. If you release the water too slowly, the boats will go nowhere. If you divide the water over too many streams then none will reach their destination. If you wait to divide the waters tomorrow, your opportunities and your workers may be gone. Thus, you must decide in spite of the unknowns.

In the end, your choices will leave some grounded and resentful, while others will rejoice and travel to new lands. This is one of the burdens and opportunities of leadership.

You must choose something you truly believe in and let the waters flow. I know the direction you must choose is within your reach. I trust that you will find your answer.

Tallis

The words of the letter hit me as truth—at least, truth for me. I always stress out about choosing a destination.

I go home each night constantly mulling over the path my department needs to choose—wondering if I am right, wondering how much damage I may create if I am wrong, wondering if I will look stupid, wondering why I don't know more, and, sometimes, wondering if I will lose my job.

Even when I am reading bedtime stories to my daughter, my mind is often miles away worrying about the right course of action. I often feel like I have gone through the motions of being home without ever fully being present.

Yet, the words of Tallis say that I don't have to carry such a load. He says choosing a destination is all about overcoming our fears of making and living with mistakes.

And, I guess he is right. How many of the things that I fear have I really seen happen to other managers? How many of the managers that I have known were ever fired for the direction they chose? The managers I know who have been fired were fired for the way they worked. (I suppose if they started firing everyone that made imperfect decisions, they wouldn't have any managers left).

So, maybe my fears are really unfounded. When it comes down to it, maybe it isn't merely the fear of losing the job that stops me. It's the fear of being wrong.

CHAPTER 10

The Advice

"Pardon my intrusion," Alfred politely speaks from across the room. "I was wondering how it was coming along?"

"Why yes, Alfred… I was just thinking about my own challenge to make decisions."

"And what have you decided?"

"I decided I don't like deciding. It always seems risky."

"Oh, quite right you are, indeed," Alfred readily agrees without any judgment. "But, if you are having trouble deciding, can you imagine what it is like for your employees? They feel lost and wonder if their actions are aligned with the goal. And, they use up a lot of your time coming back and asking you for clarity on the direction."

"That's for sure."

"May I suggest an addition to the words of Tallis that will help you put his advice into action?" Alfred offers his wisdom without any sense of superiority, and I readily accept.

"Please."

"When you get back home, would you make sure your team is clear on these questions:

- What is the purpose for this department?
- Why is this purpose important?
- Who are the people you must serve?
- What are the key things you must deliver to these people?
- What happens if you don't deliver it?
- What does success look like?

These are important concepts that should not be put off."

As Alfred begins to emphasize the need to get clear on the destination, I think of all the different mission statement experiences that I had heard of and been a part of. I think I have always seen these retreats as a form of punishment. If you are really bad you have to do a management retreat. I wouldn't be surprised if the ultimate torment used in the Tower of London was to make the condemned souls create a mission statement at some sort of retreat.

So many of the documents created at these things end up on the wall or in some file—never to be used again.

However, I resist the urge to share my cynicism and continue to listen to his advice.

"And remember, it is not just about creating some piece of paper that ends up decorating a wall and never being used," Alfred continues addressing my concerns as if he heard my thoughts. "You must create a conversation about the issues that matter most. The conversation you create is as critical as the direction. For it is through the conversation that you gain commitment and alignment."

"You're right. But, you know it is not easy to get management to agree on where they are going. How can I make a decision at my level when they haven't made a decision?"

"I'm afraid that you and everyone else are waiting for the stars to align before they take action and really decide to go somewhere. This is one of the paradoxes of leadership. You are always forced to decide without knowing. If you knew everything you needed to know, your situation would not require leadership.

"Your challenge is to do what Tallis did. You must talk to the various people involved and then decide. There is simply no getting around the issue. You own the decision.

"Come, let us go for a walk and take a break from all these thoughts before you begin the next letter," Alfred stands and we go up the stairs.

CHAPTER 11
The Second Letter

Outside, we head down the block and arrive at a small park. Alfred sits on a bench under a tree and invites me to join him. He states that way too many leaders don't create space in their life to think about what they are doing. He suggests they never find the bigger questions because they keep their head so full of things they have to do.

Without any pause, he brings me back to the letter and the importance of choosing a destination. He asks me a few questions about what I think the destination needs to be for my department. I share my thoughts and he pushes me on a few issues. He emphasizes that if I fail to take the time to get clear on the destination, I will magnify all other problems. He tells me that accepting the responsibility to choose a destination is merely the decision to accept my real job.

Our conversation meanders to other topics and after some space of time that I can't measure, we return to the bookstore. We enter the vault and a still, peaceful feeling reenters my body. Alfred provides me with the second letter without comment and he quietly leaves the room. I settle into the corner chair and start to read.

My colleague and friend,

I applaud your willingness to choose a destination. It sounds as if your workers were also grateful. Well done, my friend.

I believe your newest frustration grows from the fact that you are trying to walk two paths at once. Is it possible that you have not taken a stand on what you really value?

Just as you would not cross the desert without knowing the stars, neither can you face the paradoxes of work without knowing your values.

The demands of work will push you to do that which is advantageous or easy, yet your values will pull you to do that which is right. In those dark moments when no one is looking, when no one can hear, and when no one has to know, your values will guide you through the dilemmas of work.

When was the last time you really thought about what matters most in your life? Do you seek adventure, fame, achievement, fortune, security, or power? Each of these can be a worthy companion on your journey through life. Yet, none of them can take the place of peace of mind.

Imagine the day when the routine of work has past, and no one calls you master or asks your advice. Who is the man you wish to see in the reflection pond? The image you wish to see tomorrow will be created by the values you choose today. So, choose purposefully, my friend.

And remember, once you know your values, do not be fooled— your journey is not complete. Lofty statements are never enough. You must prove your values through actions.

Your values are tested in the midst of raging storms—where your actions can reveal your deepest beliefs. In the midst of inadequate time, competing demands, angry masters, imperfect workers, and self-serving alternatives, you will discover what you really value.

However, these dilemmas are not your enemy; they are your ally. They ask you to reveal your opinions when you want most to hide. They ask you to decide when you want most to delay. Indeed, the great opportunity of leadership is that it asks us to decide who we really are. You see, the character you develop from being a leader is as important as the results you accomplish.

Now, as you refine your values, remember the relationships that matter most in your life. Consider that your child asks not what deals you have made but rather, "Can you play?" Your parents care not how much money you can lend but rather how much time you can give them. And, your loving wife wants not to know how important you are in the marketplace but how important she is to you. They will all bless your life long after the many tasks of work have passed from memory.

I know the path you need to take is within your reach. I fully trust you will find your answer.

Tallis

The smiles of my family and friends stream across my mind as I contemplate my values. I think of playing and laughing with my family, but those aren't my only thoughts. I also think about work and my desire to make a difference. My values affect all areas of my life.

CHAPTER 12
A Recommendation

"So, when was the last time you really took time to reflect on what you stand for?" Alfred interrupts my thoughts. I didn't even know he had come back into the room.

"It has been awhile, but everyone knows I am basically a good guy," I respond a bit startled.

"That is not the question. The question has to do with what you say you value and what actions prove your declaration. You see, my good man, you and I tend to dismiss the outcomes of our behaviors because we know deep down inside what we meant to do. We can become offended because other people take things so personally. Yet, other people naturally take our actions personally because from their point of view the impact is personal. You see, we tend to discount our own behaviors and put a premium on others' behaviors.

"Let me ask you a question. If I offered you a job for a million dollars a year, would you take it?"

"Well, it depends."

"On what?"

"Well, lots of things. Where it is? What do I have to do? Who do I have to work with? What risks do I have to take? What skills would I get to develop? Is it legal? What impact will it have? How much time would I have with my family? How much travel? How secure is the job?"

"Why won't you just take the money?"

"Well, it may require me to do something I don't like or don't believe in."

"Precisely! Values drive your decisions and affect the path to your destination. You wouldn't consider making the decision without consulting your values, yet too many managers just proceed through their job without a clear foundation."

"Value setting involves making a sincere choice about who you are today and who you will become tomorrow. Not only must you be clear on your values, but just as important, you must choose specific behaviors that represent your values. You can do this for your organization as well as for yourself."

"But I don't want to impose my values on others."

"You already are. People already feel the impact of your values through your everyday behaviors. Having a conversation with your team about what matters most to you—and to them—does not impose but rather clarifies. And, just as you need to be clear on your values, the team needs to be clear on what they will stand for as individuals and as a team."

"So, how do I get started?"

"I recommend three things:

1. *Make a list of your top values.* What are the factors that really drive your actions?

2. *Write why each value is important to you.* Record the experiences of what has made this value so important in your life. The story behind the value is a key to internalizing and being able to share your commitment to others.

3. *Create a list of behaviors.* Select behaviors that would represent the achievement of each of those values in everyday life. You see, without behaviors to use as a yard stick, your values can be nothing more than a wish list. I recommend that you clarify your behaviors in the next weeks. You and your team will benefit from your efforts," Alfred states. "If you have no other questions, feel free to read the third letter from Tallis."

Alfred places the letter at the corner of the table and slowly finds a chair across the room. I am not sure whether to ask him more questions, work on my values, or begin reading the letter. My curiosity overcomes me, and I decide to read the letter.

CHAPTER 13
The Third Letter

My colleague and friend,

Your letter reminded me of my own attempts to gain commitment. I have grown old quickly because I spent too much time blaming people for their slothfulness. These many years have finally taught me that I cannot expect people to care so deeply about my needs when I am a stranger to theirs. I hope you will learn this lesson much sooner than I.

Each day you enter a marketplace full of busy people facing many demands. If you talk only when you need something, *you become a thief. If you talk only of your goals, you become a burden. If you talk only when it is convenient, you become a beggar. You must find ways to build better relationships.*

You must reach out and begin conversations with those who can complete today's duties and those who will create tomorrow's opportunities. You must learn their goals, their challenges, and their dreams.

Once you know their direction, you must be willing to continue the conversation. You see, most people ignore your requests not out of selfishness but out of desperation. Like a warm fire left unattended in a storm, good intentions are extinguished by the rains of competing demands. If you want your influence to last beyond the moment, you must return to fan the flames.

Is this not true with the rest of your life? Do you visit a friend only once? Do you hold your child only once? Do you embrace your wife only once? Do you thank God only once? No! You would never abandon such important responsibilities. You must maintain the relationships you value.

Before I go, let me leave you a word of caution. Many leaders have cast aside my words because they were uncomfortable with initiating a conversation. They tell me it is not in their nature, they fear being perceived as a peddler, or, worse, they believe starting these conversations is not honest. Experience teaches otherwise. Those who take time to build relationships create not just riches for their business but lasting friendships for their lives.

The work of leadership depends on relationships. I trust that you will find your answer.

Tallis

CHAPTER 14

The Coaching

"You know, Alfred, I already know this is the right thing to do," I call out to Alfred across the room. "But, I never seem to have time to meet with people. In fact, in my last company, we had to go through a downsizing, and, as I was getting laid off, I said that I would stay better connected in the future."

"And...?" Alfred asks, stretching his word.

"Well, I still haven't made time."

"What are you waiting for?" Alfred pokes.

"More time, I guess. Maybe I will have time when things slow down," I shrug.

"So, based on the last three years, what is the likelihood that you will have more time to do this in the future?" Alfred queries with an answer already in mind.

"Okay. I get the point. It is just hard to shift my mind into thinking it is really worth the time," I respond, knowing I am guilty, but hating to admit it.

"The challenge is to redefine your job. Your current definition of your job suggests that success is getting things done through your personal hands-on efforts. To move forward, you have to find a way to embrace the idea that you get work done through relationships, not through merely completing more tasks," Alfred emphatically states.

"But it is so hard to let go."

"Yes, but you already made that choice when you accepted the job of leader. Now, it is simply time to follow through on your decision!" Alfred makes a declaration.

I surrender to the idea. "So, where do I start?"

"Let us start by looking at how you spend your relationship time. Who are the people you spend the most time with now?"

"Well, there is Joe in Engineering, Sally in Marketing, Mark over in Materials, and of course my direct reports," I intently respond.

"Indeed, but who are the people that are the most critical to your success?"

"Well, I really need to spend more time with Linda, the VP of Operations, and some of Joe's peers, but—"

"But what?" Alfred interrupts. "What if you continue spending your time the way you are now? Would you expect to get more resources, more staff, more support from other departments, or even get a new idea through the system?"

"I believe you are right," I concede. "Nothing would change. The more I spend my work time with those who I am already comfortable with, the more my life will actually become less comfortable."

"Yes, and it isn't just about you. It affects your whole team. If you aren't connected, then their needs suffer as well," Alfred points his finger as he talks.

"But, it really isn't in my nature to go out and talk to these people," I try to excuse my behavior.

"People who are successful are not necessarily more comfortable reaching out, nor are they more blessed with an abundance of time. It is just as inconvenient to them as it is to you. The difference is where they decided long-term value will come from," Alfred begins with mild intensity and then increases his emphasis. "You believe that long-term value is in getting tasks done. They believe long-term value comes from getting the tasks done through building and maintaining relationships. They know they can't do all the work themselves. It is really just a decision about what is important."

"I guess there isn't any magic pill that is going to make me do it. I just have to start doing it." I give in to the idea that I just have to do it.

"Precisely! You can't make time, but you can make a choice about where you spend it. So to clarify your job, talk to key people who affect your work. These people may include management, customers, peers, direct reports, and vendors. And remember, you aren't surrendering your job to their will. You are simply gaining perspectives. After you understand their views, integrate the ideas and take a stand on what your real job is. Also, you may even want to consider some family members that you need to spend more time with," Alfred offers.

"I am already thinking of a few people I need to reconnect with," I respond with resolve.

"Good, start thinking about who the key people are, what their needs are, what you can do for them, and what you need from them," Alfred concludes. "And remember, this is not something you do once and then forget. You must maintain periodic contact."

Alfred really seems to think that everyone avoids this. I know I spend way too much of my time with convenient people. I wonder how my life will change if I change who I spend my time with.

CHAPTER 15
The Fourth Letter

Alfred picks up the last letter and sits down beside me. He first makes a little small talk but then asks how I am feeling with all this information. If I were at work, I would act like I had it all under control, but I know he would see right through that. So I admit it is rather daunting to be thinking of all these things.

He reminds me that there will be plenty of time to think about it when I return to work. He tells me to use the letters as a guide.

Our chat ends with his smile conveying confidence in me as he stands up. The last letter is in front of me. I take a breath and immerse myself in the words of Tallis.

My colleague and friend,

Your newest question is one of the great struggles of every leader. In fact, I still desire to do some of the daily tasks myself. It seems like it would be so much easier. Yet, doing the work myself is a luxury I cannot afford. It steals time away from the business and my future. My challenge is to create accountability within others, so we can all reach our destination. This journey begins and ends with expectations.

You see, each time you ask your workers to accept a new responsibility, you are asking them to cross a vast desert—where the sands can blind and the heat confuse. If you fail to clarify expectations, you ask your people to needlessly wander in the desert—and the desert is a cruel place to those who wander.

Expectations are like an oasis in an unforgiving desert. They tell you where you are going. They tell you where you are. They tell you when you have arrived. After all, how can an apprentice know when to work harder, when to rest, or when to seek help, if he does not know what is expected? The apprentice who must work without clear expectations is cursed like a slave to countless tasks of unknown value and duration.

And, what is more, my friend, how can you know when to celebrate, reward, correct, or even relieve a man of his employ if the expectations are not clear? Expectations create the freedom to act.

Now, as you begin sharing your expectations, beware of the temptation to act like the King of Tyre, imposing his will on his people. Setting expectations is a conversation, not a declaration. You must tailor expectations to the individuals you lead. Some will need only a destination, others will need landmarks, and still others will need to know exactly what provisions to take. And, once on their journey, you must continue to help them see beyond the mirages of competing demands by reminding them what is expected. Even the most talented worker can be fooled by the heat of the desert.

In truth, my friend, your challenge now is to let go of being master of the trade that brought you here in exchange for being master of the caravan. You must learn to trust others. You must help others trust themselves. And, just as important, you must learn to trust yourself.

Once you discover this trust, your opportunities will multiply. Providing expectations and following up creates accountability and allows you to let go, trust, and lead.

I know the path you need to take is within your reach. I trust that you will find your answer.

Tallis

CHAPTER 16
The Advice

"I have seen a lot of problems because of a lack of clear expectations," I blurt out as I finish the letter.

"For example?" Alfred responds.

"Just a few months ago, it happened to me when my boss, Heather, gave me an assignment to get a new supplier for our plastic moldings."

"Go on..." Alfred nods and encourages me to say more.

"Well, I thought for sure that I knew what she wanted, so I began the research. I spent weeks on it. But, when I showed it to her, she was surprised at my actions and the status of the project," I speak candidly.

"And, what were her assumptions about the assignment?" Alfred calmly asks.

"She thought I was bringing the data to her, so she could make the decision."

"And you?"

"I thought I was supposed to go ahead and get the ball rolling on getting a new supplier and then make the decision," I declare with both hands waving to make my point.

"What happened?" Alfred continues his calm approach.

"We worked it out and got a new supplier, but I felt like I had the rug pulled out from under me," I share my frustration but acknowledge it wasn't all her fault. "Don't get me wrong about Heather. She is a good manager. But it was pretty frustrating to think I was in charge of this when I wasn't. If I would have known up front, it would not have been so bad, but thinking you are in charge and then finding out you aren't is depressing. She should have done a better job of clarifying what was expected."

"Yes… and what were the costs of her actions?" Alfred asks.

"Well, at a minimum, I moped around for a few hours. Then I wasted time complaining to a few others. I guess the more serious problem was that the level of trust between us dropped temporarily. And, I have to say that my effort dropped," I admit.

"High costs, indeed, for both of you. Even though you are being paid to do work, pay is never enough just to be busy. People always want to know that their efforts really matter. No one wants to do something that isn't valued. We all hate feeling our time is wasted."

"That's for sure."

"So, how do you think your employees stand on the expectations you are giving them?" Alfred changes the focus of the conversation.

"I was afraid you might ask that. I have to admit that I am doing the same thing to others."

"Well then, let me give you a few crucial items to discuss when you ask employees to take on assignments. Consider each of these as a way to create clearer expectations.

1. What is the specific goal?
2. What role do you expect the person to play?
3. What relationships are critical to achieving the goal?
4. What steps must be followed?
5. How will you measure success?
6. How often and in what way do you expect updates?
7. What decision making authority does the person have?
8. What tasks are not negotiable?

"If you take even a few minutes to think through these before you give assignments, you will not only get more of the results you want, you will also reduce the number of misunderstandings." Alfred emphatically states.

"That makes sense to me, and I see that I need to do more of this for my employees. But, what do I do when my boss does not do such a good job of this?" I inquire.

"That is simple. Reverse the process," Alfred suggests.

"What do you mean?"

"Expectations are a two-way street. Both parties help to clarify them. The leader typically initiates the expectations, but the person receiving the assignment can help the leader in the process. If the leader is not providing you with the guidance, you need to ask these questions of the leader."

"Won't my boss be offended?"

"In most cases, your boss would probably be grateful. However, there are some bosses who tend to abandon employees—leaving them to figure it out on their own. Some may do this to develop you, but many do it because they are just so busy," Alfred states. "However, they all want to achieve results, so tap into their need to get results. And remember, don't fall into the same trap of making excuses about why you can't do this for your people."

A large pause fills the room. I can tell that Alfred is done sharing his insights. I wish there was something more but I know it is my turn to put the letters into action.

"Well, my good man, we have done the easy part—reading and discussing the letters," Alfred speaks more causally than before. "You now know the importance of choosing a destination, clarifying values, cultivating relationships, and creating accountability. These will serve you well if you let them. The need to answer these questions never goes away. The letters will help you find and answer the question of your time. I have placed a set of the letters in this box. They are yours to keep."

This whole experience with Alfred seems to be finishing before it began. I want him to keep talking and helping me think. I want him to tell me exactly what I need to do when I get back. I wish he would just tell me what question I need to answer. But, I guess I can never solve the real problems of my business from the safety of this vault.

Alfred reminds me to reread the letters as I search for answers. I enjoy a few more moments of enlightening conversation, but I know it is time to leave. I call to get my plane reservations changed to the next available flight. After some more chit chat, I reluctantly leave the solace of the vault and head to the airport.

CHAPTER 17
The Executive Meeting

I struggled from the moment I left London until now to determine what question our company is trying to answer—just what is the question of our time? I thought about the different letters and Alfred's suggestions. Yet, I am still searching for the questions our team needs to answer.

I hope something comes to me soon. Today we decide how we will respond to Sanlar. I wonder what I will say in the meeting.

I grab a few things from my office and head up to the conference room. I take my seat in the crowded room.

"Well, folks. You all know why we are here. So let's get down to business," Bob begins. "Margaret, will you please start with the financial forecast scenario if we don't get Sanlar's business?"

"This report outlines the financial impact to us if we lose Sanlar Technologies," Margaret, the chief financial officer, shares in a most matter-of-fact tone. "As you can see, we lose eight million dollars off the bottom line."

"How many jobs is that?" Bob queries.

"We are looking at eighty to hundred under the current assumptions," Margaret replies with exactness in her words.

"Well, that hurts," Bob speaks, rubbing his forehead.

"It's just the reality of life when you are a mid-sized company," Margaret calmly offers.

"So, Margaret, what happens if we give him the low bid?" Bob asks.

"Our rework and service costs would skyrocket. We also set ourselves up for cost-cutting requests from all other customers. We will have to use lower grade components. We go from the quality producer to the cost producer. We spend more time looking for clients because we are likely to lose clients who are not satisfied," Margaret speaks without taking a breath.

"I think I get the message," Bob interrupts.

"Just a couple more things to show the whole picture," Margaret adds. "We will be setting ourselves up to become a sales company. We will have to increase our sales staff because we will always be looking for new customers. It is a strategy used by many companies, but it never has been what we stand for. We may end up exporting some of the work. It becomes a much more complicated company."

"Thanks, Margaret. I appreciate you pulling that together so quickly. In fact, thanks to all of you for getting the numbers in on such a short time line," Bob states, then turns to our VP of Sales.

"Hank, what will it take on the sales side to make it through this if we don't get Sanlar's business?"

"We don't have any major accounts that are within three months of signing on," Hank begins without his usual flair. "The down turn in the economy has shrunk the number of smaller accounts, and the medium to larger businesses have a four to twelve month sales cycle."

"So give me the bottom line," Bob demands.

"There aren't any obvious clients that will take the place of the business Sanlar provides us," Hank shrugs as he talks. "It is not like we are off from normal business. It is just that we weren't ready for this big of a hole."

"Thanks, Hank. OK, folks. Those are our two not-so-rosy pictures of the future," Bob summarizes and then turns to me. "Stan, beyond the numbers, did your conversation with Blake provide any real insight as to what we could do to make this work?"

"First, let me just comment on Blake over at Sanlar," I begin slowly. "He is between a rock and a hard place. My relationship with Blake tells me that if the decision were merely up to him, he would go with us. But, he is not making this decision alone. The new VP is pushing to cut costs, and Blake is just as concerned as we are that the VP isn't seeing the value of our service."

The group vents at the VP's short-sightedness while I hear the words of Tallis and Alfred echoing in my brain. What is our destination? What is our purpose? What are our values?

I want to input some ideas into the group, but I am not sure if it is my place or if this is the time. On the other hand, Bob has always made a point of making sure everyone can speak freely, so I take a breath and seize the moment.

"If I could be so bold, I really think we have to ask a few bigger questions before taking any action."

"Go ahead," Bob encourages.

CHAPTER 18
The Question

All eyes look my way. The expectations in their faces make me sincerely hope I say something that will be worth everybody's time.

"I think there are many questions that we could ask—not the least of which is, 'How do we survive?' Yet, I believe we really need to ask two main questions. Once we answer these questions, we can think more clearly about what we should do," I begin assuredly on the outside, but inside I wonder where this will end up. "First, I think we need to step back and ask what we really stand for as a company. You know, who are we really as an organization?"

"You mean that values mumbo jumbo," Hank rolls his eyes as he speaks.

"If that's what you want to call it—then, yes! It may be a little cliché, but if we don't know where we stand, it is hard to make a grounded decision," I come back to Hank with uncharacteristic confidence.

"Well, OK," Hank concedes without actually believing.

"I think we need to look at what we care about." I conclude my thought and look to see if Bob is with me or not.

"You have posed a critical question—one that we, as a group, have not put on the table and struggled with for some time. I think I tend to assume we all know it, but I think it is worthy of our time to discuss what is really important," Bob begins his thought, and his words give me some validation—I asked a key question that will help us answer the bigger question in front of us.

Bob starts to share some history of the company and the values but stops mid-sentence. He stares for a moment and then tells everyone to write down what they think are the top values of the company. After a few moments, everyone begins to share their writings. The lack of consensus makes Bob grimace. It is clear that the group lacks a common understanding of the company's values.

Bob continues by explaining how values have driven major decisions in the past. Bob explicitly shares the six values that the company has held for several years: profit, quality, partnership, fairness, teamwork, and innovation. The team nods their head at each one as if they knew them all along but just couldn't remember them.

Bob asks us to discuss if these values are still viable and what it means for the company to live each value. We all break up into smaller discussions. After about ten minutes, we come back together to share our opinions. We all agree that the values are all still viable, and no changes should occur.

Bob pauses and then looks at me and says, "You said we should ask a couple of questions. What was your other question?"

"Well, the other question is where do we want to end up? You know—our destination. In three years or five years, where do we want to be? I think we can get blinded by staring only at what is in front of us for the next year. We need to think about our destination because the decisions we make at this fork in the road will put us in very different places. I know we need to survive in the short term, but what does our life look like after survival?"

Bob nods his head in agreement and then reminds us of the expectations of the Board of Directors in terms of return on investment and market share. We discuss stakeholder needs, target customers, and how we differentiate ourselves in the market. We also discuss cash flow issues and how we can actually survive in the short term.

After many heated discussions on whether or not we can survive without Sanlar's business, we come back to the reality that our values and destination haven't changed. And, in the long run, accepting Sanlar's terms would be bad for business.

Bob sums up the discussions. "I believe that our only real choice is to be willing to move forward without Sanlar's business. Does anyone want to influence me differently on that decision?" Bob invites disagreement, but we all shake our heads.

Bob then concludes, "Very well then. On Thursday, we will meet with Sanlar and try to bring them back to realistic terms. But, we will do what we need to do to keep our company moving towards its destination—even if that means losing their business. Thank you all for your hard work."

There is a sense of relief around the room because we made a decision. However, no one is more relieved than me that our discussions were productive.

CHAPTER 19
The Decision Meeting

The quiet in the room is deafening. The seconds on the clock seem like hours. Blake isn't budging on anything, and the VP of Sanlar conveniently ended up being out of the office today.

"Blake, I don't know any other way to put it," I speak in a last, hopeful breath with Bob at my side. "We value your business and want to keep working with you. However, we can't meet the price you want and provide you the quality and service you want. You haven't had any concerns with what we have delivered in the past, yet now you are making the decision based solely on price. We have run the numbers every way we can think of, and we believe we will both lose out if we provide the service at this price."

"I'm sorry, too. I have enjoyed working with you. But my VP—" Blake hesitates to avoid passing the buck. "Well, some priorities around here have changed, and I can't keep using you at the cost model you have provided. I won't take up any more of your time. But, I've got to hand it to you for sticking up for what you believe in. I wish our manage—" Blake stops mid-sentence again to avoid blaming.

There is a moment of hesitation because everyone knows that these negotiations are over. Blake states what we all know, "Well, gentleman, it looks like this isn't going to work out."

We all politely chat and begin our exit. We reach the door and Blake turns slowly as if he wishes we would say something else. For a guy who just got a lower price by going with another company, it seems that his trophy is more of a burden than benefit.

Bob and I look at each other but say nothing as we walk out to the car. I feel a sense of fear envelop my whole soul.

Now, we are sure to lay some people off. I try to remind myself that we did the right thing. All I can see in my mind is the face of my coworkers who will have to tell their kids and spouses that they just lost their job. I guess I could get canned just as easily as anyone else. The thought of telling my wife that our plans for a better house will have to be put on hold is dreadful. I can't imagine the burden on Bob.

As Bob and I get in the car, I remember the words of Tallis:

Your values are tested in the midst of the raging storms—where your actions can reveal your deepest beliefs… However, these dilemmas are not your enemy; they are your ally. Letter #2

CHAPTER 20

The Mistakes

I am finally at the point of getting my team focused on a destination. But, it hasn't been easy. The decision to drop Sanlar Technologies sent a shock wave through our company. Rumors, layoffs, accusations, and long meetings have been the norm for the last ten weeks. Keeping people engaged has been very tough.

To get my team focused, I reviewed the letters for clues, and I found that a few of the words of Tallis matched my situation:

To create the future, I had to make more time for it. I had to move from reacting to the everyday tasks that kept me busy to initiating conversations that gave me insight. Letter #1

With this in mind, I invested time in talking with executives, managers, employees, vendors, and customers to get a feel for priorities. As a result, I pushed for my Operations team and the Engineering team to work together to mutually define where we should go. We jointly came up with goals and gained agreement on how we would work together. It was a lot of work, but I think it is going to pay off.

After choosing the destination, I spent more time clarifying and reclarifying this new direction with my own team. In fact, I may have over done it.

One of my employees passed me in the hall this morning and restated the direction before I said anything. I think he was afraid I would tell him again if he didn't tell me first. However, there are no complaints about too much clarity.

I have definitely made progress since meeting Alfred, but I haven't mastered applying all the letters.

"Hi, Stan. This is Joan in accounting," she begins in a deliberate tone over the phone. "I was paying one of your vendors, and I wasn't sure which account you are putting this to."

"What is it, and how much is it?" I respond with no concern.

"It's some type of equipment for $53,753.85."

"What?! Fifty-three thousand dollars?! Who in the world spent that much money?" I release my true feelings without hesitation. "Oops. Sorry, Joan. Nothing personal. I know it isn't you."

"The approver on this is John Cormack," she responds as if my outburst meant nothing.

"Thanks, I need to get back to you. I'll call you back later today. Good-bye."

I get John in my office, and we discuss his actions. I am angry at him for putting me in such a bad position with the budget. We talk and it becomes painfully clear that my definition of empowerment and his are quite different. I feel like he should have known better, but then the words of Tallis came to me:

Expectations are an oasis in an unforgiving desert... The apprentice who must work without clear expectations is cursed like a slave... Expectations create the freedom to act. Letter #4

I apologize to John for not clarifying my expectations. We discuss the goals, roles, decision-making authority, and processes that I expect. And now, just a few minutes later, we seem to have a shared understanding.

I just wish I would have taken the time to do this when I first gave out the assignment. I thought John would understand what I meant. But, now that I think about it, I was just avoiding my responsibility to clarify.

John shares his ideas on why the equipment is going to make a difference. We discuss his proposal, and I actually think he is right about the impact. I just wish I would have known about it sooner.

John walks out of my office and the words of Tallis once again come to mind: *The journey begins and ends with expectations. Letter #4*

CHAPTER 21
The Pay Off

It finally happened. After seven months of overanalyzing situations, solving everybody's problems, and trying to know everything, I discovered something important—I am not everyone's answer.

Now, when things get crazy, I step back and ask a basic question: what question are we really trying to answer?

In fact, my employees are getting used to the idea that they need to come prepared to respond to a problem—rather than expect me to provide an answer; although, I think it would be a lot quicker sometimes to just tell them what to do.

I think I have made the switch from working "in" the business to working "on" the business, and, even though I have made a few financial and political mistakes, I seem more able to live with my decisions. I think I'm beginning to understand what Tallis said:

Once I learned that I could survive the consequences of my choices, I became free to learn the lessons—both good and bad—of my experiences. Letter #1

Although I can't say that the feeling of faking it is totally gone, it feels different now. It is more like *confident* faking instead of unconfident faking. It works better for me. In fact, some days I have to admit that I am making a difference.

"Hey, Stan. You got a minute?" Dan inquires hurriedly with frustration in his voice.

"Sure. But, I need to warn you. I am expecting a short call, so we might get interrupted."

"Not a problem."

"What's the panic about?"

"Engineering dropped the ball. Again!"

"What do you mean?"

"They promised to have the specs to us by last week. They still haven't delivered them. Now, we have had the prototype production line sitting idle because we had it scheduled for the new product. But... no specs."

"Say more," I respond and resist the temptation to start providing advice.

"I can't get Engineering to keep their commitments. They are always promising and never delivering. Why is it these people keep falling through? Can you talk with their manager and get her to put some heat under those guys?"

I temporarily ignore his request and begin to tactfully ask what he understands about Engineering's situation—their goals, pressures, obstacles, timelines, and needs—and what he has done to keep in touch. We talk and the words of Tallis come to my mind:

Most people ignore your requests not out of selfishness but out of desperation. Like a warm fire left unattended in a storm, good intentions are extinguished by the rains of competing demands. If you want your influence to last beyond the moment, you must return to fan the flames. Letter #3

I resist quoting the letters to Dan, but I can see that he really hasn't done much to build or maintain the relationship. My phone rings and the caller ID says it is Blake.

"Excuse me, Dan. It is Blake from Sanlar—this is the call I told you about."

"Go ahead."

"Hi, Blake. Thanks for calling me back," I am glad to get a hold of Blake again.

"Sure, happy to," Blake responds.

"Great, how did your family adventure to the beach go?" I follow up from our last call.

"Just fine, but I think we still have beach sand in the car."

"Yeah, I know how that goes… Say, I was just following up on our conversation last month about the challenges you have faced with the new vendor."

"Let me tell you, it hasn't been a very fun party—lots of rework," Blake shares.

"What is your VP thinking these days?" I probe.

"I think he knows he was wrong. He is definitely not getting the cost savings he dreamed of. The amount of rework we have had has sent overtime through the roof. Anyway, it may be too late for him. There are rumors about him being let go," Blake speaks more candidly than seven months ago.

"Well, I wish I could act more disappointed," I laugh as I speak.

"No need to. It has been a rough ride."

"Well, I was wondering if you gained any insights from the process you have gone through with this vendor that you could pass on to us that might make us better?" I ask with the hope of getting at some deep issues.

"Well, I'd be glad to share some thoughts, but can you give me a little time to think about that?"

"Sure. How would you feel about having lunch sometime in the next month?" I ask.

"That would be nice. Give me a call the first week of the month," Blake replies.

"OK. I will call you then," I finish the phone call.

"Sorry about taking that call, Dan. I've been trying to keep in the loop with Blake, but we usually end up playing phone tag," I reconnect with Dan.

"Not a problem. You warned me about the call anyway," Dan politely responds.

"So, tell me more about what you have done to build and maintain the relationship with Engineering," I begin where we left off.

"You know, Stan, I think it is pretty obvious to me now what I need to do," Dan responds without answering my question.

"What do you mean?"

"Your phone call said it all," Dan begins. "You have been staying connected with Blake over all these months, even though you didn't have to. I have been expecting Engineering to come to me. I haven't done my part to stay connected. I think I know what I need to do."

Dan walks out and he seems satisfied that he got what he came for, and I feel sure that I am beginning to understanding what Tallis taught:

> *Those who take time to build relationships create not just riches for their business but lasting friendships for their lives. The work of leadership depends on relationships. Letter #3*

CHAPTER 22
The Celebration

Tonight I am free from worrying about any questions or answers. The only thing I care about tonight is having a good time.

After eleven months of intensity, I can push the pause button on work and enjoy our annual company party. The ballroom is filled with decorations, colleagues, anticipation, and energy.

I find my seat. Everyone gives Bob a big round of applause as he takes the microphone in his hand.

"Thank you. But really, it is all of you who deserve the applause," Bob begins with his heart full of appreciation for everyone. "In the last year, I have seen focus and dedication unlike anything this company has ever known. We have become more effective on the things that matter most. It's been great to see us all come together.

"So, let me unveil the figures for the year. Ladies and gentlemen, because of your efforts we were able to... break even!" Bob pauses as everyone cheers and applauds. He then adds, "I don't think I have ever been so happy to not make money."

Bob continues his praises for the group, and his true, unabashed pride in everyone shows through his eyes. At times, I think he is ready to shed a few tears as he gives his personal thanks for what everyone has done. He continues on.

"Now let me share just one more bit of great news. Today I received a call from Sanlar Technology saying they want to renew their contract with us on our terms," Bob tries to continue, but the cheers prevent him. The crowd yells, whistles, and applauds at the news. "When we get their business back, this is going to make for one great year."

Everyone cheers again, and Bob concludes his remarks, steps down, and moves through the crowd. Everyone compliments him on his speech. After a few minutes, he makes his way over to me.

"Hello, Stan."

"Well done, Bob. You said just what needed to be said. And wow, Blake called you up?" I say with a grin because Blake called me earlier in the day.

"Yes, it seems someone was keeping in contact with him periodically during the last year. You wouldn't know anything about that would you?" Bob laughs.

"Well, I might have known something about him calling today."

"Thanks, Stan. You and I both know you were a key person in pulling this together."

"Well thanks. It took a lot of people."

"Oh, quit being so humble. Let's face it. You got the company focused on where we needed to go," Bob says. "You know, you gave differently to this than the other managers. Everyone sees it, and they find it easy to follow you."

"Thanks," I accept his words with some reluctance. The conversation pauses, but then Bob continues.

"Stan, I have one more thing. We are going in some new directions as a company. I believe we are ready again to expand into the southern region. I need a new general manager to run that operation. I want you to head it up."

"Well, I'm speechless. That is quite a leap. I really feel like I have just barely got a handle on what I am doing here. I have so much more to learn in this role."

"Oh, I have no doubt you could do more in your current job, but I can't think of anyone else in the organization that I would rather have guiding the new group. I have talked with the board, my team, and your boss, and we all agree—and that was before they knew about Sanlar coming back."

"Wow! But, I'm not sure I'm ready to make that big of a jump."

"Oh, blast! You weren't ready the last time we promoted you either, but that hasn't seemed to matter!"

"Well…" I hesitate.

"Well nothing. Be in my office first thing Monday morning and let me know your decision," Bob emphatically states and moves on to be with others.

I am dazed thinking about Bob's offer. I thought tonight would be free of difficult questions. Wow, was I ever wrong.

CHAPTER 23
The Next Step

I arrived at work early this morning to finalize my decision. Although my wife and I talked at home for hours over the weekend, I'm still not totally sure what to do.

As I make my way to my desk, I begin debating with myself if I can really do this. Maybe I succeeded in my current job because it was actually an easy task—anybody could have done it. Maybe my team succeeded in spite of me. I just stayed out of the way and let them do their jobs. Maybe I was just lucky—and the luck will run out. What if I can't actually do this again? But, the fact is, we did succeed.

I pause from my mental detour and see the old book on my desk—the one I originally found with the telegram in it. I pick it up and an envelope drops from its pages. It is from Alfred. He must have slipped it in before I left London. I open the letter and begin to read.

Stan,

You have found this letter because you have reached a turning point—a small moment between confidence and doubt, a time when you wonder if you are prepared for the challenges ahead. Please consider this one final lesson.

When you are a leader, it is easy to be blinded by the need for safety, stability, validation, money, and praise. However, these things are concerned with what you want to take from your job. They are not the job. If you wish to find confidence in leading, you must ask yourself, 'What do I really want to give?'

You possess a unique combination of expertise, perspective, and hope. When you give these gifts, you create the power to change the world—and yourself.

Take time to consider those things that matter most in your life.

- *What do you care deeply about at home, at work, and in the community?*

- *What values, talents, and abilities do you want to contribute?*

- *What future do you want to create?*

When you give to these questions, you will find energy and freedom. When you give to these questions, you will move beyond the criticism and doubts. When you give to these questions, you will learn to answer the question of your time—not just for today, but for a lifetime.

To make a difference, you simply need to take the next step— your next step. Give of yourself and you will be successful on any path you choose.

I trust you will find your answer.

Your friend and colleague,

Alfred

I feel like Alfred is sitting next to me telling me I am ready. I stand up and head to Bob's office. I am fully aware I will be thrown beyond my experience—and way beyond my comfort zone. I guess I wouldn't have it any other way.

TELEGRAPH

TO Dear Leader.

Your presence requested at

www.davejennings.com.

History affected by your

decision. Bring the book.

Alfred

Alfred's Notebook

You must find

the question of your time.

FIND THE QUESTION

What problem are you trying to solve? Are you sure this is the real problem?

Why is this problem so important? What is at risk? (Organizationally, professionally, personally)

What do you fear will happen if you don't take action? What do you fear will happen if you do take action?

What information or resources do you need to move forward?

You create the future

you make time for.

CHOOSE A DESTINATION

What future do you want to create?

Why is it important to arrive there?

What information do you need to make
a decision?

What are you spending time on instead of
choosing a destination? Can you afford this
in the long run?

Just as you would not cross

the desert without knowing the stars,

you cannot face the paradoxes of work

without knowing your values.

CLARIFY VALUES

What values do you aspire to live by?

What values do you currently live by?

Who can give you an honest assessment of your stated values and your outward behaviors?

What value conflicts are you currently experiencing?

What do you need that will help you resolve these conflicts?

You must reach out
and begin conversations
with those who can complete today's duties
and those who will create
tomorrow's opportunities.
You must learn their goals,
their challenges, and their dreams.

CULTIVATE RELATIONSHIPS

Who are the people that are key to your success?

What are their goals, pressures, obstacles, timelines, and needs?

Who are the people you need to spend more time with?

Who are the people you need to spend less time with?

What are three changes you need to make in how you spend your time?

*Doing the work yourself
is a luxury you cannot afford.*

CREATE ACCOUNTABILITY

What expectations do you have for your people? How do you know they understand the expectations?

How are you measuring success? Do your people really understand how you measure success?

How often and in what way do you expect your people to update you? Do they know this? Who do you need to follow up with right now?

What are you doing to really show appreciation for results? Do your people value this type of appreciation?

*You possess a unique combination
of expertise, perspective,
and hope.*

*When you give these gifts,
you create the power to change the world—
and yourself.*

COMMIT TO GIVING

What do you care deeply about?

What values do you want to see fulfilled?
What talents and abilities do you want
to give?

What do you need to let go of so you can
give more? (A task, a belief, a doubt, a
skill, or a responsibility)

Why is it important for you to be leading
in this position at this time?

What needs to happen next?

Once you learn that you will survive

the consequences of your choices,

You are free to learn the lessons
—both good and bad—
of your experiences.

MY NEXT STEPS

_____

_____

_____

_____

_____

_____

_____

_____

_____

_____

_____

_____

_____

ABOUT THE AUTHOR

DAVE JENNINGS IS KNOWN AS a catalyst who accelerates leaders' impact in situations that are beyond their experience. Using performance psychology, he instigates, he questions, and he uncovers the real barriers so leaders can face their incompetence and accept their real job.

Dave knows the emotional psychology inside leadership. In the trenches with executives implementing global strategic change initiatives in complex organizations, he understands the risks, stresses, and opportunities. He has coached, trained, prodded, and cajoled thousands of leaders and high-potentials from blue-chip companies such as Deloitte, Intel, ExxonMobil, Hewlett-Packard, and Microsoft.

At Intel, his prodding led to $12M savings in one conversation. At Microsoft, his partnership in change initiatives led to breakthroughs that facilitated the launch of half billion dollar projects, achieved awards, and returned millions of dollars. His change management framework at the software giant was adopted world-wide.

With a PhD in Sport Psychology and emphasis in Organizational Psychology, he knows the world of accelerating impact. His doctorial research tested the tools of resilience on a most at-risk group: uneducated women in dead-end jobs. The impact was immediate and lasted far beyond expectations. His findings set the foundation for his passion to research how leaders lead in complex, high-stakes situations. As Associate Professor in Organizational Leadership and Strategy in the #1 ranked MBA program of Brigham Young University, he continued his research in leader transition and organizational change.

Before helping leaders step up their performance, Dave knew what it meant to step up his own in the competitive world of ballroom dancing. Dave was a national champion and toured world-wide. He has passed the torch to his daughters who compete in local and national events.

From ballroom dancing, to women in dead-end jobs, to advising large scale transformations in blue-chip companies, Dave has made a surprising discovery: to continually succeed, performers, athletes and leaders all must adopt skills that are scalable across multiple situations. Their mindset and skill set must rise to meet the constant unknowns of the environment.

ABOUT BUSINESS ACUMEN, INC.

BUSINESS ACUMEN, INC., provides world-class solutions for aligning strategy and leadership. Working with many Fortune 500s, midsize firms, and government, Business Acumen understands the challenges, risks, and opportunities of leading complex organizations.

Business Acumen creates high impact solutions for clients by:

- Analyzing strategic options and leadership opportunities.
- Creating and facilitating high stake retreats and meetings
- Building comprehensive leadership development systems
- Designing and implementing organizational change initiatives
- Providing executive and management coaching

Learn more at: **www.business-acumen.com**

CONTINUE THE LEARNING

PUT THE *CATAPULTED* CONCEPTS to work in your organization. Visit our website and learn more about ways to continue your journey to success.

- **Keynote Addresses.** Bring the *Catapulted* concepts to your next conference. Each presentation is customized to meet the needs of your audience.

- **Strategic Retreats.** Work with one of our consultants to create a high impact retreat.

- **Seminars and Training.** Attend one of our highly interactive programs either at your worksite or at one of our public sessions.

- **One-on-One Coaching:** Customize the *Catapulted* principles to your specific situation by working with a coach.

- **Leadership Development Systems:** Apply a whole-system approach to developing leaders in your organization.

Keep growing your skills. Take advantage of the tools and resources available to you and your organization.

Obtain more information at: **www.davejennings.com**

CATAPULTED: THE SEMINAR

MAKE THE PRINCIPLES OF *CATAPULTED* come alive in your every day life. Attend the live seminar and gain these benefits:

- **IDENTIFY** the key question of your leadership challenge
- **INCREASE** employee engagement
- **ACCELERATE** your leadership learning curve
- **INCREASE** your credibility and confidence
- **EXPAND** your strategic relationships
- **MANAGE** your boss more effectively
- **CREATE** accountability within your team

This high-impact program goes beyond giving you good ideas. It provides a new mindset and skill set that you can use throughout your career.

You can bring this program inside your company or attend a public session. One-on-one coaching is also available.

Obtain more information at: **www.davejennings.com**

SHARE YOUR STORY

You can make a difference in the world by sharing your catapulted story. We collect leader experiences to advance research and improve people's lives. It doesn't matter if it is a big leap or a small step. We want to hear your story.

Tell us about your experience:

- What was it like when you were catapulted beyond your experience?

- What doubts and hopes did you have? What mistakes did you make? What successes did you achieve?

- What do you wish you knew when you where being catapulted?

- What advice can you pass on?

The challenges, the political dynamics, the personalities, and the time pressures make your experience unique.

"Three of my top employees quit within a month of me accepting this job."

"I went from managing a highly technical product to managing a bunch of independently minded engineers."

"I went from managing one product to being the VP."

"I didn't even want the job of supervisor, but they needed someone to take it on."

"I left my secure corporate job and started my own company."

"I went from managing 5 people to 300 overnight."

Your experience could make someone else's challenge easier. Share your story at: **www.davejennings.com/mystory**

COMPLETE THE LEADERSHIP ASSESSMENT

DEAR LEADER,

As a bonus for investing in Catapulted, I invite you to complete the complimentary online leadership assessment. This assessment is a great way to determine where you are on your leadership journey.

The Catapulted Leadership Assessment can help you:

- Evaluate your performance for each of the letters from Tallis.
- Determine your strengths and opportunities.
- Identify next steps to increase your impact.

Just go to **www.catapultedleader.com/bookbonus**.

Best regards,

Dave Jennings

Printed in the USA
CPSIA information can be obtained
at www.ICGtesting.com
LVHW091515080824
787695LV00001B/127